Melodies of Faith

Melodies of Faith

AN ADVENT DEVOTIONAL FOR AFRICAN AMERICAN CHURCHES AND FAMILIES

written by
AFRICAN AMERICAN SCHOLARS, PASTORS, AND LAY LEADERS

compiled by
CHARISSE L. GILLETT

edited by
TANYA J. TYLER

chalice
PRESS

Print: 9780827223844

EPUB: 9780827223851

EPDF: 9780827223868

ChalicePress.com

Printed in the United States of America

TABLE OF CONTENTS

Introduction

The sounds, spirit, aromas, and feelings of hope, peace, joy, and love that permeate Advent, Christmas, and Epiphany come together powerfully in scripture and music. *MELODIES OF FAITH: An Advent Devotional for African American Churches and Families* was inspired by this sentiment. We wanted to share favorite songs of the season to help you prepare for Advent, celebrate Christmas, and embrace all the possibilities of Epiphany.

Guiding Scripture

Now in that same region there were shepherds living in the fields, keeping watch over their flock by night. Then an angel of the Lord stood before them, and the glory of the Lord shone around them, and they were terrified. But the angel said to them, "Do not be afraid, for see, I am bringing you good news of great joy for all the people: To you is born this day in the city of David a Savior, who is the Messiah, the Lord. This will be a sign for you: You will find a child wrapped in bands of cloth and lying in a manger." And suddenly there was with the angel a multitude of the heavenly host, praising God and saying, "Glory to God in the highest heaven, and on earth peace among those whom God favors!" [Luke 2:8-14] [NRSV Updated]

The contributors engaged this beloved scripture from their perspectives as African American people of faith. They mined their personal histories to connect that faith with their cherished memories and music of Christmas. These memories include a flicker of light piercing the midnight sky of Alabama; the love of words that inspires spirit and intellect; the taste of hard candy. The songs include spirituals that gave the ancestors courage – "Rise Up, Shepherd, and Follow" and "Sweet Little Jesus Boy"; the traditional – "O Come All Ye Faithful" and "Hark! The Herald Angels Sing"; and the modern and contemporary – "Santa Claus, Go Straight to The Ghetto" and "Mary, Did You Know?" The music is in conversation with the scripture, and our prayer is that both are in dialogue with your individual and collective faith journeys.

We invite you to actively engage the material and receive the reflection questions to evoke table conversations at home and church. Pray along with us that someday at Christmas, we will see with our own eyes that all God's promises have come true. And with the angels, we will rejoice and sing!

From all of us to all of you,

Happy Advent

Merry Christmas

Wonderful Epiphany

ADVENT WEEK 1

SUNDAY

A Litany for Advent

While we were yet sinners, Jesus came at the right time ...

During Advent, the whole church, the Body of Christ, looks forward to the second coming of the promised Messiah ...

As the Word made flesh, Jesus came to an unprepared people in an unprepared place.

We remember our Savior's humble, obscure entry into our world.

God, we remember Your love for Your creation and thank You for Jesus, Your only begotten Son.

God, help us understand and appreciate the ways in which You use the forgotten, the marginalized, the outcast, the weak, the poor, the imprisoned, and the afflicted to proclaim Your kingdom. ...

Lord Jesus, as we reflect upon the joyous miracle of Your birth, deepen our understanding of the purpose of Your coming ...

We herald Your coming, Wonderful Counselor. You are the King of kings, Lord of lords, the Mighty God, Everlasting Father, the Prince of Peace. ... You alone are worthy of all our praise!

Rev. Dr. Dolores Carpenter
General Editor, The African American Heritage Hymnal

MONDAY

Hope in the Darkness

... the stars are brightly shining ...

Darkness can be the portent of many things. A child might be afraid of the dark, convinced that monsters lurk unseen, waiting for the lights to go out to pounce. Often darkness or nighttime is construed in myriad symbolic ways. Night can be associated with death, destruction, and captivity. Sometimes it is a spiritual darkness.

Luke's account finds us with the shepherds one dark night as they are watching their sheep. Let's use our sacred imagination: Do you feel the cold stillness? Do you see the stars? Can you hear the sheep baaing? When the angel of the Lord appears, can you sense the terror the shepherds must feel at such an otherworldly sight? Can you sense their wonder as they hear the angel's news and watch the subsequent heavenly celebration?

"O Holy Night," written by the French poet Placide Cappeau in the 19th century, brings this story to vivid life. It has always been my favorite carol. I love it because of the beautiful way the words and music illustrate that Gospel message. As we approach the Advent season, it's not difficult to see that the country – indeed the world – is in a state of chaotic, cruel darkness. But lest we fall into despair, we must remember it was in a similarly dark time God sent our Savior to us. Even though we may weep in the night, Jesus comes in the midnight hour to bring us the hope we so desperately need.

Reflection: What act of kindness can you undertake to bring light to someone experiencing a dark time?

Prayer: Dear Divine Source of Light, help us see beyond what looks to be a time of impenetrable night. Remind us that through Your Son, we will forever have light and love in the world. Amen.

Rev. Tracey L. Anderson-Tellado, Corpus Christi, TX
Regional Moderator, Christian Church (Disciples of Christ)
in the Southwest

TUESDAY

The Tools to Teach and Reach Change

Prepare ye the Way of the Lord ...

In my college years, two and a half generations ago, one of the favorite albums on campus was the soundtrack to the Broadway musical *Godspell.* From the mid-1950s to the early 1970s, the time of my formation and educational and spiritual growth, we experienced violence, confrontation, fear, loss, anger, sadness. Growing up with the world at war on TV and daily demonstrations leading to the assassinations of civil rights leaders and spokespersons, my generation was challenged to understand the possibilities of creative hopeful change. For me and many other young people, hope was alive in the insistent creativity of the arts.

On the *Godspell* soundtrack, we heard the shofar calling people into community. The prelude, "Prepare Ye the Way of the Lord," could be heard shouting the good news out of dozens of windows on campus. It was hard not to rejoice in the hopeful song. Everyone listened to the gospel songs – Christians and people of Jewish background alike, and also international students and people who knew more about confrontation and demonstration than faith, hope, and possibility as the tools to teach and reach change.

Times are still challenging. Change remains difficult in our culture. Inclusion, compassion, equity, and justice – the message of the Gospel – are still hard to achieve. But we, hard-working people deeply rooted in commitments of faith, are called every year to announce a time of making ready, re-opening possibility, and hope. Advent is the season of preparation. Even after decades and centuries, even after a difficult past year, here we are again, preparing the way for the work of the Kingdom.

Reflection: What are the lyrics of hope that keep you connected and committed to the work of faithful action?

Prayer: Creator of Life, keep us awake and alert. Help us keep our lanterns burning as we prepare with hope for the challenging days ahead. Amen.

Rev. Dr. Claudia Highbaugh, Pomona, CA
Retired Dean of Religious Life, Connecticut College

WEDNESDAY

New Birth

The first noel, the angel did say ...

I grew up in the Black Belt of Alabama, the cradle of the Civil Rights Movement. I always looked forward to Christmas. I was fascinated when I saw the Christmas carols booklet in the Montgomery *Advertiser.* One of the songs that caught my attention was "The First Noel." As a child, I didn't understand the meaning of the word "Noel." I looked it up and discovered it is a French word derived from Latin meaning "birthday" or "new birth." It can refer to the entire Christmas season or the good news of Jesus' birth.

The first "Noel" was sung by an angelic chorus to a group of poor shepherds. Ever since, we have been singing, "Noel! Good news! A new king is born, bringing new birth for all." During this Advent season, I encourage everyone to declare to the broken village in which we live the glorious news, just as the angels did. As you sing "The First Noel" this Christmas, let it remind you that the King of Israel, the Lamb of God, the Alpha and Omega, the Beginning and the End, the One who is the same yesterday, today, and forever, has been born.

Reflection: In this season of celebrating the birth of Jesus, what new birth are you witnessing?

Prayer: Creator God, help us remember the birth of Jesus so we may share in the songs of the angels. Amen.

Rev. Dr. Dale Braxton, Fort Deposit, AL
Associate Regional Minister, Christian Church (Disciples of Christ)
in Alabama Northwest Florida

THURSDAY

Found by the One Born to Give Us Life

... singing a song with water in my eyes ...

James Brown, one of the most influential soul music singers in history, was on to something when he released the song "Santa Claus, Go Straight to the Ghetto" in 1968. Brown was adamant that our Black boys and girls would not be forgotten, marginalized, or downcast during this transformative season. The song asks Santa Claus to "hook up your reindeer, fill every stocking you find," to go to impoverished communities and bring light and love. Brown declared, "I know what you will see because that was once me" – echoing a vision that life does not begin and end in the ghetto.

Jesus was born on the margins of dominant religious and patriarchal structures. The angel declared, "You will find the Babe wrapped in bands of cloth, lying in a manger." The Baby would be found in the most obscure place economically, socially, and systematically. He would be found where no one chooses to go or live. He would be found in places of despair, giving hope. He would be found in a place without dignity, yet He would give dignity to those who wanted it. It is good to be found by the One born to give us life! God will come get us, bring us out, and set us on the path of life.

Reflection: How can communities in poverty gain dignity and rise above the dominant culture that seeks to keep them stagnant?

Prayer: Dear God, thank You that the ghetto cannot hold back gifts of dignity, worth, and eternal life found in You. Thank You for coming to us and giving us the gift of liberation. Amen.

Rev. Dr. Nadine Burton, Brownsburg, IN
Vice President, Great Lakes Region, Christian Church Foundation

Because of What I Know, I Can Sing

Mary, did you know that your Baby would one day walk on water ... ?

Each year Christmas music floods the radio, and for a brief period I hear all my favorite songs playing on an unending loop. "Joy to the World," "Now Behold the Lamb," and my favorite, "Mary, Did You Know?" The haunting words of this carol live within me the entire season and beyond.

What does a mother think when she looks upon a sleeping child that requires everything of her to live, grow, and develop? The helplessness and innocence of that child call her to a deep and fierce posture attuned to every need, every hurt, every possibility. Mama is ready!

What was Mary thinking when she looked upon her child? He would walk on water, heal the blind, and make us all new. What did Mary think when she realized *her* child, the child she delivered, would someday deliver *her?*

In this season of hope, joy, peace, and love, we are reminded that we *do* know. We do know that Mary's child came to deliver all of us. We do know that the child Mary held, loved, protected, and helped nurture into manhood became the Lamb of God.

Reflection: How does this song help you connect with Mary as a person of faith? As an African American parent?

Prayer: Dear holy and wise God, we give thanks for the obedience and faith of Mary. Amen.

Dr. Charisse L. Gillett, Versailles, KY
President, Lexington Theological Seminary

SATURDAY

A Shepherd for the Shattered

... in fields where they lay keeping their sheep ...

My friend, a veterinary scientist, told me there is only one other living creature who has as much trouble with stress as we humans do: sheep. For sheep to avoid stress, my friend said, they need a shepherd.

The occupation of shepherd was a thankless job – difficult, dangerous, and dirty. The shepherd had to stay awake all night to guard the fold. And yet, God chose shepherds – who could not observe the strict religious practices nor follow the meticulous hand washings and ceremonial regulations of the day – to be the first to receive the good news of the birth of Christ. The annunciation of the birth of the Savior came not to important dignitaries but to shepherds tending their flocks. An angel of the Lord stood before them and said, "Do not be afraid; for see, I am bringing you good news of great joy." God gave an angelic announcement for the shepherds' pathetic predicament. The first will be last and the last will be first. God will reverse what we have been through. God will light up the dark places in our lives. God will turn negatives into positives. God will add glory to our story. God will bring joy to the world!

Reflection: How do you find and maintain your joy in this world?

Prayer: Holy Creator, thank You for the witness of the shepherds. Indeed, You are a Shepherd for the Shattered. Amen.

Rev. Dr. William E. Crowder, Homewood, IL
Senior Pastor, Park Manor Christian Church
(Disciples of Christ),Chicago, IL

ADVENT WEEK 2

SUNDAY

Come, Lord Jesus, Come!

Emmanuel shall come to thee ...

In our common daily lives, people move with such speed yet are not going anywhere. I have seen places where people are moving but there appears to be nothing in sight. Even in this season where we celebrate the birth of our Lord and Savior, there is darkness and uncertainty, fear and trepidation. The hymn writer pleads: *"O come, Emmanuel, and ransom captive Israel that mourns in lonely exile here until the Son of God appear."*

Come, Lord Jesus, as the promise moves to reality. Come, Lord Jesus, for we know that what You have done in real human history, in real human lives, You can do and are doing in the lives of people now. Come, Lord Jesus, even in the midst of the stark reality of a world dominated by oppression and injustice. Come once again to "ransom captive Israel."

Reflection: Are you moving too fast to appreciate how the Lord appears in your life today?

Prayer: Lord, come just as You came before. We stand waiting and trusting that redemption, fulfillment, wholeness, and peace will come. Amen.

Rev. Dr. Donald K. Gillett II, Versailles, KY
Regional Minister, Christian Church In Kentucky

MONDAY

A Multitude Sang Out

New life, new hope, new joy He brings ...

Seeing a newborn child inspires wonder. Most people blessed to behold an infant soon after its birth are awestruck and humbled by the emergence of a new life. Even an ordinary birth is a miracle. But imagine seeing an Infant whose life will change the world!

I remember the first time I heard the song "Jesus, Oh, What a Wonderful Child" in church. The choir processed into the sanctuary, marching to the beat, swaying side to side, belting out the lyrics. It was powerful, emotional, and moving. It stirred something in me that opened my eyes to the scriptures about Jesus' birth. Luke 2:8-14 says a multitude of the heavenly host sang out, praising God. That doesn't happen at every birth, no matter how adorable the child might be.

There is a key ingredient in this scripture that connects this new life to joy: *hope*. The birth of Jesus is much more than His humble beginnings suggest. It is about the whole world and how it is about to change. Jesus' birth is about the access we *all* have to new life because of *His* life. This is what the angel heralds and what the heavenly host proclaims. Our world is fallen and fragmented. We feel broken, inadequate, wounded. But Christ brings hope that inspires us to realize we are loved by God. That hope shows us our brokenness can be repaired. It transforms our lives of lack and inadequacy into lives of abundance and compassion, and our woundedness receives healing. We recognize God calls us to spread Christ's love and make a difference in the world.

Reflection: How does Jesus' birth inspire you to make a difference in the world?

Prayer: Our prayer, O God, is for new life, new hope, and new joy this season. Amen.

Rev. B. Christopher Dorsey, Indianapolis, IN
President, Disciples Home Missions

TUESDAY

We Didn't Know

... they made You be born in a manger ...

The lyricist who wrote "Sweet Little Jesus Boy" was not a member of the community that offered their faith in dialectic spirituals. From the vantage point of privilege, he captured the soul-stirring reality of unbridled faith. It is the quiet hum of the ancient ones peering from an unknown corner in the universe, petitioning for compassion and mercy. It is the birthing of hope in the midst of oppression. Through the lens of the marginalized and disempowered living on the outskirts of acceptable society, heaven whispered eternity's revelation – the good news of great joy for *all* people.

How did the ancestors – the wounded-womb offspring of the lowly and disenfranchised – see so clearly what others failed to recognize? Was the plight of this holy child evident through their sense of rejection and degradation? With the Christ Child, they formed an impromptu affinity group, comrades wrapped in strips of cloth and denied any sense of royalty.

How strange to discern an apology from the ones who were not perpetrators but were yoked in the kindred spirit of "other," familiar with the pain and suffering of the dispossessed. *"Just seems like we can't do right. Look how we treated You."* The reverberating question is, if we know, will we become the embodiment of God's generosity as we see the Holy Child anew? Sweet little Jesus boy, surely we must know.

Reflection: Are there acts of omission and commission you might seek forgiveness for this season?

Prayer: Creator God, give us strength in the face of oppression and courage and hope in the face of the unknown. Amen.

Rev. Marilyn S. Fiddmont, Spring, TX
Vice President, Southwest Zone, Christian Church Foundation

WEDNESDAY

A Call to Freedom

There's a star in the East on Christmas morn ...
So begins a hymn sung by enslaved African Americans dating back to at least 1867 (post-Civil War) but most probably composed long before. "Rise Up, Shepherd, and Follow" could be construed as a call to action, to freedom from common activities, just as the shepherds were called to witness the fulfillment of a significant promise in scripture. Shepherding was a necessary and important vocation. But it is by far superseded by the salvific arrival of the Christ Child!

The Advent season allows us to reflect upon the fulfillment of God's promise of redemption from our current life plights and from our tattered relationships with a Sovereign God. We find fulfillment to the life we need and desire. It's a call from the mundane task of herding sheep to the worship of the Great Shepherd. Just as enslaved Africans Americans felt a movement towards God's redemption in Jesus, let us not wallow in the concerns of the present age but revel in the realization of God's love.

It is easy to get caught up in our day-to-day routines. But as disciples of the Redeemer of our souls, our mandate is to seek Him and follow His call upon our lives. Humble shepherds received the call that night 2,000 years ago and responded by going to find Christ. Won't *you* rise up, shepherd, and follow?

Reflection: In what ways have you felt a movement towards God's redemption in your life? In the world? In your community?

Prayer: Wise Sovereign God, You have redeemed us and made us whole. Let us, like our ancestors, remember in this Advent season to be hopeful. Amen.

Rev. Kenneth Golphin, Lexington, KY
Presiding Elder, Lexington District AME Church, KY

THURSDAY

Anticipation

Tiny tots, with their eyes all aglow ...

I was born and raised in Mississippi. I can testify there are two kinds of dark: city dark and country dark. I grew up in the capital city of Jackson, so even on summer nights, the streetlights and house lights provided enough illumination for us children to continue playing outside. I sometimes visited my grandfather in the Mississippi Delta. He lived on a gravel road with no street signs or light posts. When night fell, unless you had a flashlight or lamp, you could not see your hand in front of your face. That country is *dark*.

Country dark is not just a physical manifestation. It is spiritual as well. The political and theological outlook for first-century Palestinian Hebrews was dark. Their ancestors had lived and died waiting for the Messiah. Into this darkness, this dreary reality, an angel appeared and brought a message of hope and light – "good news of great joy." The wait was over! The Messiah was here! The angel told the shepherds where to find this light that had come into the world. I am sure as they searched, their hearts were filled with anticipation.

Nat "King" Cole did not write "The Christmas Song," but his version is so iconic that it is essentially his song. The lyrics touch all your senses with anticipation. You can smell the chestnuts roasting on the open fire and the turkey cooking in the oven. You can feel the frost nipping at your nose. You can hear the choir singing. You can see the children's eyes "all aglow." They waited all year, in symbolic darkness, and now the moment is upon them. The wait was worth it.

Reflection: How has an angel appeared to you, guiding you into the light away from darkness?

Prayer: Our prayer is that you rejoice in the season and the light it brings. Amen.

Rev. Jesse Jackson Jr., Spencer, OK
Pastor, East Sixth Street Christian Church (Disciples of Christ),
Spencer, OK

FRIDAY

God Uses the Unlikely to Share the Good News

... let us all with one accord sing praises to our heavenly Lord
...

One of my beloved Christmas season traditions is watching *A Charlie Brown Christmas*. Our hapless hero, Charlie Brown, has been tasked with securing the tree for the Christmas pageant. It sounds simple enough, but if you know Charlie Brown, the result will be anything but simple. He chooses what could be called a twig more than a tree. It is small and has few branches, and even a slight touch causes the needles to fall off. Charlie Brown is lambasted by his friends for his choice. Overcome by all the commercialism they exhibit, he yells, "Does anybody know what Christmas is all about?" In response, Linus, after dropping his security blanket, recites the words of the Luke passage.

Linus, Charlie Brown, and the author of the beloved hymn "The First Noel" remind us that the glamour and glitz we have associated with Christmas is not an authentic expression of the birth of Jesus. His birth was announced to a group of shepherds who were simply going about their daily lives. Many of us are like shepherds: We go through our day barely being recognized or acknowledged. But God sees the worth in those whom society would deem "the least of these," and it is to them God chooses to bring the good news: "Noel, born is the king of Israel!"

Reflection: In what ways has God chosen you to bring the good news to others this Christmas season?

Prayer: Thank You, God, for choosing the simple and the least to bring Your good news of salvation and peace. Amen.

Rev. Dr. Amariah McIntosh, Bowling Green, OH
Senior Pastor, Phillips Chapel CME Church, Akron, OH
Associate Director, Ohio Council of Churches

SATURDAY

An Announcement!

My world is filled with cheer and you this Christmas ...

I served a small congregation in southwest Virginia. The little community has a population of less than 5,000. I learned during my brief time there about coal miners who risked their lives working days and nights in dark tunnels and tiny crawl spaces miles beneath the Blue Ridge mountains. In that darkness, fear and fragility are real. Cognizance of "this day" became more evident to me during my tenure there. Even today, Donny Hathaway's performance of "This Christmas" has, for me, a feel of an "announcement" to it.

Luke's Gospel describes a dark night in the fields of Judea. In the presence of a glowing light, the first words of the angel to the shepherds arrested their fear: "For to you is born this day ... a Savior." An angelic announcement brought good news to these humble laborers living at their worksite and managing their tasks by moonlight. It marked "this day" as holy – set apart from all those before it and all those that would follow it. The angel's announcement of Jesus' birth was a Kairos moment. It was God's Incarnation, Jesus the Word made flesh, wrapped in bands of cloth. In the praise and worship of a heavenly host, there came an announcement that God's eternal glory had intervened into the midst of human history, that "this day" God's Messiah, the Anointed One, had come into the world to liberate the lowly and the least, those considered "expendable" by this world.

Reflection: What is your responsibility to your community to actualize the hope, peace, joy, and love of God's Incarnation proclaimed in the songs of Advent/Christmas/Epiphany?

Prayer: Merciful God, thank You for the promises of eternal hope, peace, joy, and love so prominently proclaimed in the seasons of Advent and Christmas and for their manifestation in Your Son, Jesus, in the season of Epiphany. Amen.

Rev. Dr. Marcus L. Leathers, Washington, DC
Regional Minister, Christian Church (Disciples of Christ), Capital Area

ADVENT WEEK 3

SUNDAY

Hark!

With the angelic host proclaim ...

The first word of the opening stanza of my favorite Advent hymn has, over the years, arrested my attention and has given me focus during this season. The word "hark" calls us to listen. It is followed by an exclamation point that suggests the one who calls to us is passionate about the request. Angels are always singing. Our challenge is to set our souls to the right frequency so we can hear them.

Howard Thurman has been instrumental in helping me hear angels sing. In his book, *The Moods of Christmas*, Thurman writes, "There must be always in every man's life some place for the singing of angels." This place is more spiritual than geographical. We need to intentionally provide space in our heads and hearts for the singing of angels.

If angels are always singing, why don't we hear their song? Advent is filled with so much noise: preparing our gift list, menus, travel itineraries, Christmas play rehearsals, cantatas, office parties, endless trips to the mall. There is the noise of heavier-than-usual traffic and long checkout lines. There is the noise of gun violence, insufficient finances to cover that gift list, grief, death, and birth.

This Advent, I gently say to you, retreat to that place in you where you can hear angels sing anew: "Glory to the newborn King! Peace on Earth and mercy mild."

Reflection: How do I reserve a place in my head and heart for the singing of angels?

Prayer: Gracious God, help me open that place within me today so I may hear angels sing. Amen.

Rev. Dr. William L. Lee, Roanoke, VA
Chair of the Board of Trustees, Lexington Theological Seminary

MONDAY

Rise and Shine and Give God the Glory!

Follow the Star of Bethlehem ...

The clarion call was the same every day: *Rise and shine! Let's get to it!* My mother was not kidding when it came to getting the four of us children up and moving. Monday through Friday: out of bed; teeth brushed; face washed; dressed and to the breakfast table before school. On Saturday, the call prepared the way for chores, chores, chores. There was an added verse on Sunday mornings: *Rise and shine and give God the glory!* And we were off to church!

The plantation Christmas carol, "Rise Up, Shepherd, and Follow," was the clarion call of the angel to the shepherds on Christmas morn. The message was clear: Leave everything behind and follow the star to Bethlehem. On the late 19th-century slave plantations in the South, this carol delivered a hopeful message to the enslaved community: Follow the star in the East to freedom and a new life. For us, it is a reminder to rise and shine and give God the glory every day.

Reflection: How does this song and other Negro spirituals help prepare you for the coming of Jesus?

Prayer: O God, bless us each day as we remember to rise and shine and give You the glory! Amen.

Rev. Dr. Belva Brown Jordan, Claremont, CA
Interim Executive Director, Disciples Seminary Foundation

TUESDAY

I, Too, Can Sing

Won't you listen to the angels sing ...

I have some fond memories of growing up in Huntsville, Alabama. One of these is of the St. Luke Missionary Baptist Church #2 Choir singing "Jesus, Oh, What A Wonderful Child." The whole church would – as we say in the Black Church – "go in" on that song! It seemed something would intensify every time the refrain was repeated and the words, "New life, new hope to all He brings" rang out all around the church. Although we didn't formally observe Advent, we knew and celebrated the significance of the new life and hope connected to the first coming of our Christ.

"Jesus, Oh, What A Wonderful Child" was not the song's original title. When it was recorded in 1952 by Margaret Wells Allison and the Angelic Gospel Singers, its title was "Glory to the Newborn King." Several revisions of the song have been released over the years. However, the last words of the refrain have remained the same: "Glory, glory, glory to the newborn king."

When I reflect on the difference The King has made in my life, I, too, can sing, "Glory to the newborn king" with the angels who sang on the night of His birth. When I consider the new opportunities The King has prepared for me, I, too, can sing, "Glory to the newborn king." When I contemplate The King's second coming, I, too can sing, "Glory to the newborn king." Regardless of what version or revision of life you're in this Advent, you, too, can sing, "Glory to the newborn king."

Reflection: With all the challenges facing us as African Americans on a daily basis, how does your connection with Christ keep you filled with hope, peace, joy, and love?

Prayer: Lord, grant us glimpses of Your excellence and goodness this Advent season. With these glimpses, fill us with hope, peace, joy, and love as we celebrate Christ our King. Amen.

Rev. Dr. Nathl L. Moore, Georgetown, KY
Pastor, First African Baptist Church, Lexington, KY

WEDNESDAY

We Worship You!

O, come, let us adore Him ...

I long to experience great hope this Advent season. I invite you to come into His presence and adore Him. God's presence brings unspeakable joy as we celebrate the glory we have received.

Come, let us kneel before Him! We have a Shepherd who keeps watch over us during the night. There is always an invitation to come and bow down before Him. Jesus brings us hope so there is no need be afraid of what awaits us. He is here to guide us and prepare us to receive the good news of His birth.

Come, let us worship and adore Him! The angels are praising God, saying, "Glory to God in the highest heaven, and on earth peace among those whom God favors."

Reflection: How will you adore Jesus this Advent season?

Prayer: Loving God, we long to be in Your presence. Help us draw closer to You. Connect us in bringing the good news of Your love and to those around us. Amen.

Rev. Dr. Syvoskia Bray Pope, Louisville, KY
Pastor, New Century Fellowship Christian Church (Disciples of Christ),
Louisville, KY

THURSDAY

How Wonderful to Wonder and Wander

... for poor ordinary sinners like you and like I ...

I am a word geek. Part of my daily devotion is to not only read something that will lift and challenge me spiritually, but I also check various websites for the "word of the day." Etymology was one of my favorite courses in high school. I'm still enamored with English and bask in the study of literature, particularly figurative language, i.e. similes, personification, and onomatopoeia (*Boom! Crash! Clunk!*). Alliteration brings me jubilation and joy. I don't find correct grammar to be a grave endeavor ; it grounds great growth of mind (see what I just did there?).

When I first heard Mahalia Jackson sing "I Wonder as I Wander," I was just as astounded by her vocal performance as by the alliterative title itself. The song is a homophone of Advent proportions. It is an invitation to imagine, dream, and allow our creative juices to flow and overflow. As the shepherds wondered about the meaning of singing angels and pondered shining glory, so, too, this song beckons us to think anew concerning the "ordinary" and "poor." Advent presents an opportunity to contemplate novelty and the "not yet."

The companion of wondering is wandering – to journey without a particular destination. The shepherds are comfortably "out under the sky" until angels come to agitate their silence and elicit angst and terror. The Holy One has a way of causing dis-ease in places of the most unlikely solace. Perhaps that's the point. Some parts of our journey *should* rattle and dishevel us. The shepherds' terror at the sight of the angels perhaps was more to remind them – and us – that the weary wonder and stillness of night need not lull us into spiritual, professional, or communal sleep. Darkness ought not deter us from the wandering or journey that calls us. We are called to wonder as we wander – wherever we are going.

Reflection: How often do you allow yourself the freedom to let your mind wonder freely?

Prayer: To the One whose glory cracks through the heavens to meet us dwelling out under the sky, thank You for being our Wandering Companion. You are indeed a Wonder to our wandering, seeking, searching souls. Amen.

Rev. Dr. Stephanie Buckhanon Crowder, Homewood, IL
Professor of New Testament and Culture
Director, ACTS DMin in Preaching Program,
Chicago Theological Seminary, Chicago, IL

FRIDAY

"Hallelujah!"

There's a blaze of light in every word ...

Canadian singer, composer, and musician Leonard Cohen originally released "Hallelujah" on his album *Various Positions* in 1984. The song achieved little success until John Cale covered it in 1991. Rolling Stone named it among the "500 Greatest Songs of All Time." Cale's version was featured in the hit movie *Shrek*, but Cohen's is my favorite. His deep, raspy voice seems to penetrate my whole being, calling me to unfettered praise of God. Cohen sings of a secret chord David played, a song that incorporated "minor falls" and "majors lifts," imaging a baffled king writing "Hallelujah, hallelujah, hallelujah," because it was all he could – or needed to – sing.

Some say this is not a Christmas song. I say it is – and more. "Hallelujah" is a song of praise about real life and love. Christmas is all about love! Love stories rise and fall; they repeat, they end, they never end. They lift us to better places in ourselves and they give us pain that breaks us. Love stories call us out of old things and into new things – out of unholy things into holy things. The angel comes to the shepherds with "good news." The angel calls them (us) into a new narrative that will be of great joy for all people. Other angels join in the hallelujahs. Our praise lifts us out of old things and calls us into new things. There was indeed a secret chord ... Jesus, the Messiah, the Lord. Sing it with David and the angels: Hallelujah!

Reflection: What makes you sing hallelujah?

Prayer: Dear God, hear our hallelujahs as we offer You praise for sending the Savior, which is Christ the Lord. Keep us ever singing His glory! Amen.

Rev. Joan Bell-Haynes, Macon, GA
Interim Regional Minister, Christian Church In Georgia

SATURDAY

In the Silence of the Night

... sleep in heavenly peace ...

Many years ago, there was a young girl who, every Christmas Eve, had great expectations of Jesus appearing to her in the silence of the night. Late in the night, after all the caroling had stopped, all the lights were turned off, and everyone else was asleep, she would get out of her bed and move to her window. With a child's faith, believing in miracles, she waited for the heavens to open and Jesus to appear. Standing, waiting, watching the heavens, she would hum her favorite carol, "Silent Night."

Year after year, around that midnight hour, the young girl went to her bedroom window. Believing miracles can happen, standing there, knowing *this* would be the year she would have a glimpse of Jesus in all His glory. She waited to welcome Jesus with an open heart and outstretched arms.

Many years have gone by. Now she knows she does not need to look to heaven to find Jesus. He is already within her, guiding her with His light and His love.

Funny though, even as she has now grown up, there are still times on Christmas Eve that, with the heart of a child, she briefly glances to the heavens. Just in case Jesus shows up, she wants to be there!

Reflection: Have you identified when you best hear from God?

Prayer: Lord God, with the faith of a child, may we always remember if we listen, we will hear from You. It just may be during the silent times in our lives. Amen.

Mrs. Jackie Compton Bunch, Columbus, OH
Lay Leader, Christian Church (Disciples of Christ)

ADVENT WEEK 4

SUNDAY

A Litany for Christmas

... This is the good news: The Anointed Messiah has come ...

Thank You, God, for the gift of Your Son, Jesus, the light in darkness and hope of the world ... .

His name shall be called Emmanuel, meaning, "God is with us."

"Do not be afraid, for I am bringing you good news of great joy for all people, for to you is born this day in the city of David a Savior, who is the Messiah, the Lord."

With all the angels, we praise Your Name and tell the world the wondrous story of Your birth.

"Sweet little Jesus boy, born in a manger. Sweet little holy child, we didn't know who You was."

... You came with power that we may share Your power; humble that the poor and lowly might see their greatness; destined for a cross that all might have life eternal.

God so loved the world that [God] gave [God's] only begotten Son.

The work of Christmas is to find the lost, heal the broken, feed the hungry, release the captives, rebuild the nations, bring peace among the people, and make music in the heart.

Come celebrate ... ! [Sing] glory to the newborn King! "O come, let us adore Him, Christ the Lord."

Rev. Dr. Dolores Carpenter
General Editor, The African American Heritage Hymnal

MONDAY

An Invitation to Participate

... let loving hearts enthrone Him ...

Shepherds, often marginalized and overlooked, were invited to witness the miracle of the Savior's birth and actively participate in God's unfolding plan. Imagine the sheer surprise and uncontainable joy the shepherds felt when the angel appeared, inviting them to see the child born in the city of David.

As we sing "What Child is This?" we, like the shepherds, are invited to reflect on the profound significance of this child sleeping on Mary's lap. This child carries within Him the power to transform the world. He brings peace to a world at war, hope for the despairing, and justice to the oppressed. The global community is deeply scarred by injustice, poverty, and suffering. War, human rights violations, and systemic inequalities persist. The birth of Jesus ushers in a new era of inclusion, justice, and compassion. Just as the angels proclaimed peace on earth at Jesus' birth, we are called to work together for a global community where all realize justice and equality. As we join our voices in singing, "This, this is Christ the King," let us remember Jesus came to transform our society, bring peace, and inspire us to action. Let us strive to be peacemakers and advocates for the voiceless. Let us, guided by our faith, commit to taking concrete action to promote peace and justice around the world.

Reflection: How can we fully embrace the angelic declaration of peace on earth and goodwill toward all this Advent season?

Prayer: Gracious God, help us embrace the message of peace and justice proclaimed at the birth of Your Son. Amen.

Rev. Dr. LaMarco Cable, Indianapolis, IN
President, Disciples Global Mission

TUESDAY

Without the Ones We Love

Now I stand all alone and my house is not a home ...

The tune is light and has an oddly joyful rhythm, but upon listening to the words, one hears the mournfulness. "Christmas just ain't Christmas without the one you love." I recall hearing the O'Jays singing this song and thinking, "That's not Christmas-y. Why are we listening to this song of lost love?" My sister would have said, "It's deeper than that – listen again."

Christmas is often filled with laughter, fun, and joy. Our traditions and gatherings with families, friends, and colleagues are purposefully celebratory with food, Secret Santas, and multiple trips to the mall. We're expected to embrace the spirit of joy that infuses the season. But Christmas just ain't Christmas without the the ones we love. The mournfulness of the song is ever present when we are living on this side of glory without them. The sadness of the holiday season can be overwhelming for those whose memories of Christmas include lost love, painful goodbyes, and death.

The scripture tells us, "Do not be afraid." The celebration of the Christ Child does not take away our human pain, but it gives us hope because we know we will experience love again. It gives us hope because we know we will someday celebrate with those who have gone on to glory. In the darkness of the fields, good news was delivered.

Reflection: Consider who is missing from the celebrations in your place of employment and at church and family gatherings. How can you honor the memories of their lives with hope, peace, joy, and love?

Prayer: Good and wise God, we are grateful for music that helps us remember those no longer in our earthly orbit. We celebrate our memories of them today. Amen.

Dr. Charisse L. Gillett, Versailles, KY
President, Lexington Theological Seminary

WEDNESDAY

Preparing for a Wider Joy

Lift up thy voice with strength – lift it up, be not afraid ...

Pathways to joy are chronicled by disciples and proclaimed by angels. Joy is not an accidental discovery or an acquisition intended solely for private consumption. The biblical canon cast it as a gift from God and a fruit of the spirit. *Handel's Messiah: A Soulful Celebration* reinterprets the masterful oratorio by George Handel and the genius of divine joy for a new time. Originally composed to celebrate Easter, the *Messiah* gained a wider audience as Christmas liturgy. Through African American musical idioms, joy is decoded and reinterpreted with new harmonies.

Disrupted by glory, shepherds and frontline watchers in neighborhoods and churches, schools, and hospitals halt their midnight walks. Advent is the season of extraordinary proclamation and communal revelation, where untold glory finds a ready witness and unexpected hearing finds a faithful multitude. It is not an invitation to naïve hearing or muted praise or reluctant messages. It's a gift that disrupts our routines and re-positions our attention to glad tidings and a wider joy beyond our own making.

The Advent season invites us to lay our burdens and safeguards down. The antidote to terror and fear is joy spoken, sung, and witnessed. It is not merely an idea or an idol. It will not distract, overwhelm, harm or destroy. Joy will open up new vistas for storytelling, holy hearing, and the glory of God for all.

Reflection: Where is joy being decoded and expanded in your community this season?

Prayer: God, move us from glory to glory, from private joy to a wider joy in service of all. Amen.

Rev. Yvonne T. Gilmore, Columbus, OH
Chief of Staff, Office of the General Minister and President, Christian
Church (Disciples of Christ) in the United States and Canada

THURSDAY

Profound Hope

It's been a long time coming ...

Sam Cooke's mournful lament, "A Change Is Gonna Come" is not a common entry on lists of favorite Christmas songs. However, woven into the eloquent poetry of his words, Cooke captures the meaning of Christmas with a message of profound hope. In the song, Cooke looks at his circumstances and acknowledges his inability to reconcile his theological beliefs, his connections to community, and the actions of those who should be closest to him. Cooke is not alone in his view of the world as inconsistent and unreliable. Luke, the writer of our focus text, joins Cooke in his contextual analysis – and his hope.

Luke is writing to the church of his day. Some scholars believe by the time this gospel was written, the Roman Empire had gone through a succession of emperors and Jerusalem and the temple had been destroyed. Most of the original disciples had been martyred. A new generation had been born while the church was waiting for the second coming of Christ.

Luke begins sharing the message of profound hope for the church by pointing to the experience of the shepherds. The angels arrive to deliver a targeted message to them. First, they communicate to shepherds and to the church that God is aware of who you are, where you are, and all that is happening around you. Second, the changes around you are part of God's "Good News." The shepherds are told to look for the validation of their hope. God will come to you in forms you don't expect (an infant, not a king), in places you do not expect (a manger, not a palace), doing what you do not expect (welcoming shepherds, not holding court).

We don't know how Cooke's hope was validated. But the complicated inconsistencies of his context don't make him waver in his profound hope. Cooke understands change is eminent and underway. The last stanza let us know his hope was affirmed. There were times he thought he couldn't last much longer, but now he's able to carry on. It had been a long time, but he knew a change was gonna come. *Oh, yes, it will.*

Reflection: Am I willing to act with profound hope until I see changes?

Prayer: Loving God, sometimes I cannot make sense of the world around me. Help me each day seek new strength to act and the profound hope to believe. Amen.

Rev. Vinnetta Golphin-Wilkerson, Taylorsville, UT
Co-Moderator, Central Rocky Mountain Region

FRIDAY

"Go Tell It!"

... over the hills and everywhere ...

The African American spiritual "Go Tell It on the Mountain" echoes the experience told in Luke, about angels that suddenly accosted shepherds tending sheep in the fields. Shepherds were invisible and unempowered people. The angel's divine message of good news told the shepherds of the arrival of peace, favor, and joy. Salvation had become a reality through the birth of Jesus Christ. After the shepherds' encounter with the angels, they overcame their fear and took courage to "go tell it!"

African American spirituals brought hope to the enslaved ancestors living a daily reality of anguish and destroyed dreams. They, too, were invisible and unempowered. "Go Tell It on the Mountain," brought to life by John Wesley Work Jr. and the Fisk Jubilee Singers, resounds with the good news that the birth of Jesus Christ will break the yoke of oppression and bring God's liberation and salvation. The spirituals empowered enslaved African Americans to embrace hope in a God who liberates and saves.

Reflection: How did the shepherds and enslaved African Americans overcome fear to become bold new carriers of the message of hope and liberation?

Prayer: Lord, help us shake off timidity and raise our voices to proclaim the good news of hope in Jesus. Give us the courage to "go tell it!" Amen.

Rev. Dr. Denise Bell, Lexington, KY
The Donald and Lillian Nunnelly Chair of Pastoral Leadership,
Lexington Theological Seminary

CHRISTMAS EVE & CHRISTMAS

Let Us Go Now and See

A Christmas Eve Candlelight Communion Service

Call to Worship

Take yourself out of this current reality and imagine yourself in a field outside Bethlehem, under the night sky. Pretend you are a shepherd, huddled with your fellow sheep tenders around a fire. Feel the flames warming your chilled fingers. Gaze at the burning wood, watching as the sparks fly upward. Gather your cloak closer around your shoulders as the wind blows. Hear the familiar nighttime noises. The bleating of the lambs. A wolf's howl! Take a firmer grip on your shepherd's staff. Sniff the air. You smell wool, grass, dirt. There's nothing out of the ordinary. Just another long dark night in the fields. Glance up at the sky. There are stars ... the moon with its rays of light reaching out across the darkness. Soon the shimmer of sunlight will come over the horizon. Savor the silence. Be at peace with the peace. All is calm, all is bright.

Opening Hymn "Let All Mortal Flesh Keep Silence"

Lighting the Candle of Hope

The first candle we light is the candle of hope. There is not enough darkness in all the world to put out the light of one single candle. Hope leads the way. We are grateful for the Candle of Hope, knowing it will illuminate our path to God.

Song "O Come, O Come Emmanuel"

Scripture *Luke 2:1-5*

Lighting the Candle of Peace

More than the absence of war, the Peace of God passes all understanding. It is warmth and comfort, as well as courage and conviction. Peace is the key to God's kingdom. Let us light the Candle of Peace with gratitude for God's mercy and strength.

Song "O Little Town of Bethlehem"

Scripture *Luke 2:6-7*

Lighting the Candle of Joy

The joy of new life and new possibilities is surging in our souls tonight. When we think of how much God has given us, we cannot help but find a wellspring of joy in our hearts. May the light of the Candle of Joy shine in and upon us forevermore.

Song "The First Noel"

Scripture *Luke 2:8-14*

Lighting the Candle of Love

Christmas is all about love: God's love for us. Christ's love for us. The love we have in return for both. For God so loved the world that God sent Jesus to us. May God's love shine through us to light and warm the world.

Song "While Shepherds Watched Their Flocks"

Scripture *Luke 2:15-20*

Invitation to Communion

How appropriate that shepherds were the first to hear of the birth of the Good Shepherd ... the One who has come to gather us into His loving fold, to heal us and help us, to care for us and even lay His life down for us. All followers of Christ, regardless of church affiliation, are invited to share at the Lord's Table on this holy night, taking the Bread and the Cup in remembrance of Jesus the Messiah. Christ came so that we can return to God for forgiveness, love, and redemption. Let us remember, rejoice, and celebrate.

Song "What Child Is This?"

Words of Institution

Sharing Communion

Lighting the Christ Candle

The people who walked in darkness have seen a great light. Those who lived in a land of deep darkness – on them light has shined. *Isaiah 9:2*

Sharing the Light of Christ

Let us create a circle of hope, peace, joy, and love around the sanctuary. We will pass the light from the Christ Candle to each other as we sing "Silent Night."

Song "Silent Night, Holy Night"

Benediction *John 1:1-5*

Walk in the light as He is in the light. Christ is born. Christ is risen. Christ will return. Alleluia! Go in hope, peace, joy, and love. Amen.

CHRISTMAS DAY

And in despair I bowed my head ...

How can anyone be cynical and satirical on Christmas Day, of all days? Yet in his poem, "I Heard the Bells on Christmas Day," Henry Wadsworth Longfellow decried how he found no joy in the jubilant tintinnabulation of church bells. His mind was on the situation in the world at the time: war, not peace; hate, not love; darkness, not light. And in despair he bowed his head.

Indeed, Christmas is not always a happy time for everyone. Although we are urged to be jolly and sing and celebrate, for some this may be the first year they are coping with the loss of someone near and dear to them. It may be the first time they are alone after a breakup or divorce. They may be in a new city where they have no friends with whom to share the holiday. And there are many, many people who are struggling to survive the horror and deprivation of war. How can they rejoice under such circumstances?

And yet ... We believe this is the season of peace. We believe this is the season of hope. We believe this is the season of love. We believe this is the season of joy. That is why Jesus Christ was born: to show us the way to peace. To reawaken our spirits to hope. To teach us to love and care for one another. To bring us everlasting joy. To bring light where there is darkness. To let us know better, brighter days lie ahead. Yes, the weary world is in sad shape right now. But ... someday at Christmas ...

Reflection: Do you know someone who is having a hard time getting into the "Christmas spirit"? What can you do to help them see the light of hope?

Prayer: Dear God, help me overcome any inkling of darkness and despair that tries to steal the hope, peace, love, and joy I have found in Christ the Savior. Amen.

Rev. Tanya J. Tyler, Alto, NM
Pastor, First Christian Church (Disciples of Christ), Ruidoso, NM

CHRISTMASTIDE

SECOND DAY OF CHRISTMAS

This Joy We Have

Shepherds, why this jubilee?

In moment-by-moment installments, on screens and devices, we are reminded people live in fear. Gun violence, food insecurity, escalating housing costs, and discrimination masquerade as inevitabilities. When fear is the factor driving our existence, many will conclude individual well-being and familial safety are assured when we retreat to our own networks.

Yet, as we absorb Luke's Christmas text, we reach the transformative truth that the presence of God neutralizes fear. Speaking to shepherds who were terrified by the glory of God in their midst, an angel assured them: "Do not be afraid ... I am bringing you good news of great joy."

Jesus, Emmanuel (God with us) breaks the chains of fear that imprison our imaginations and hold hostage our hopes. In Christ, we are new people whose lives go beyond the boundaries of happiness and into the realm of renewable and sustaining joy! Though election outcomes may be outrageous, policy enactments may prove egregious, and court decisions may be dreadful, we still possess joy!

Reflection: How does joy fuel your faith and witness?

Prayer: Magnificent God, we praise You that in Christ the chains of fear are now broken. Joy to the world, the Lord Jesus Christ is come! Amen.

Rev. Dr. Jack Sullivan Jr., Columbus, OH
Executive Director, Ohio Council of Churches

THIRD DAY OF CHRISTMAS

Terrified Yet Hopeful

... for mighty dread had seized their troubled minds ...

Have you ever braced yourself to hear bad news – taking a deep breath, clenching your fists, prepared to hear the worst? Have you had moments you knew could change your life but didn't yet know how?

The shepherds were in the fields minding their own business when there was a great interruption in the sky! Their first response was fear. They saw an angel and the glory of the Lord around them and they were terrified. I do not know how I might have reacted upon seeing an angel in front of me and perceiving the glory of the Lord around me. I would like to think I would have a deep sense of peace and wonder. But maybe I would also be terrified, and honestly, that's OK. There are times in our lives when we are worried, nervous or scared. We brace ourselves for the worst, yet deep inside we hope for the best. We hope to be assured by an angel or a friend or our pastor that things are about to change. We desperately need to hear what the angel said to the shepherds: "Do not be afraid; for see, I am bringing you good news of great joy."

May you brace yourself for good news even when there are strange interruptions!

Reflection: How do you handle unexpected moments of fear and joy?

Prayer: Lord, I pray that even when I am terrified, I will expect and experience good news. Amen.

Rev. Dr. Delesslyn A. Kennebrew, St. Joseph, MO
Associate General Minister of the Christian Church (Disciples of Christ)

FOURTH DAY OF CHRISTMAS

Light Into Darkness

... You stepped down into darkness ...

Christmas Eve at Ruby Clark's House was a sight to behold. My grandmother, affectionately known as "Momma," loved Christmas and made Christmas Eve a family affair not to be missed. Momma began shopping for Christmas the day after Christmas to make sure she had gifts for all. She prepared cakes, pies, and homemade candy for weeks leading up to Christmas Eve. Momma wanted her family together on Christmas Eve, so we came in our cars or by cab or by Chicago Transit Authority bus or train. Regardless of the mode of transportation, Momma's children, their children, and their children showed up for Christmas Eve. There was light even in dark times.

I think about this year – the darkness that permeates so many neighborhoods and homes; the devastation brought by wars, poverty, and being unhoused; the shattered family situations. I wonder how light is found in darkness. Momma has gone on to be with the Lord and the family no longer gathers for the Christmas Eve extravaganza. However, there is still light born from the struggles and joys experienced through the faith of a grandmother from Shannon, Mississippi. Momma understood how Jesus pierced the darkness of His times and continues to do so today.

Reflection: What traditions does your family have that honor the spirit of Christmas light shining into darkness?

Prayer: Dear God, help us remember the faith of our mothers and fathers. Remind us that even in the darkest times, light will always win. Amen.

Rev. Dr. Donald K. Gillett II, Versailles, KY
Regional Minister, Christian Church In Kentucky

Holy Travelers Migrating in the Night

... and when temptations press thee near ...

Saturday nights were considered sacred and holy when I was growing up. They included ironing clothes, prepping tomorrow's dinner, and rereading our Sunday school lesson in preparation for worship. Today, I boldly testify the spiritual preparation I received is worth its weight in gold. It offered discipline and a readiness for twenty-first-century ministry. Filled with two generations of African Americans migrating from the deep South, our church gathered weekly with a holy reassurance that "whatever happened the night before would not hinder the good news from arriving Sunday morning."

To model this belief, we often sang songs expressing our faith in action. "Dark Was the Night, Cold Was the Ground" was a congregational favorite. First written in 1792 by a clergyperson and remade in 1927 by a blues singer from Alabama, the song intersected with those who traveled far and faced much. The lyrics reminded them that any fear of darkness could not prevail. Not dissuaded by the "night," the travelers moved forward. Another perspective insists God is standing by to offer light and safety to those en route. The story of the Black Migration traveled from the rich, fertile soil of Alabama's "Black Belt" and now travels throughout me.

The angel of the Lord traveled to bring the good news of Jesus' arrival. The announcement of His birth removed barriers that spelled unholy nights. Nestled in His arrival was a freedom to walk in the night with a conviction that offers firmness of faith. Wherever you are, may your migration lead you toward knowing the God of love and light through Jesus Christ.

Reflection: Can gratitude and praise help lead and guide you toward your new destination of safety and grace?

Prayer: Lord, thank You for strengthening us as You strengthened our ancestors. We praise You for this generation and for the generations arriving. Amen.

Rev. Dr. Christal L. Williams, Brownsburg, IN
Regional Minister, Christian Church in Indiana

SIXTH DAY OF CHRISTMAS

A Hard Candy Christmas

I won't let sorrow bring me way down ...

The Elders of the church insisted each person, especially the children and teens, leave Christmas service with a paper bag filled with hard candy, fruit and nuts, and a small gift. Assembling the bags was part of the preparations for our celebrations. The Elders insisted the bag be brown, not a cheery red or sparkling green, and certainly not one of those fancy gift bags.

The bag and its contents were symbols of a time when the abundance of the season appeared in brown paper. They were signs of history and hope for futures that would be.

"Hard Candy Christmas," written by Carol Hall and popularized by Dolly Parton, is a brown paper bag of memories reminding us of the tangible struggles many people face at Christmas. The song is a call to resist defeat and be tenaciously hopeful about the future despite one's circumstances. Each year, the Elders of the church reminded us with a brown paper bag that the child born in the manger is a sign that God is with us always.

Reflection: Has your journey included a hard candy Christmas? How do you keep the lessons of that time in your life relevant?

Prayer: Knowing God, we express gratitude for the signs and symbols that call us to remember the past and the promise of our future.

Dr. Charisse L. Gillett, Versailles, KY
President, Lexington Theological Seminary

SEVENTH DAY OF CHRISTMAS

Calling On Jesus

Children, love has arrived ...

"Jesus," written by KEM and featuring Patti Labelle and Ronald Isley, touches my heart and spirit. It shares the narrative of the birth of Jesus Christ. It says heaven was satisfied there would be peace on earth because of Jesus' birth. KEM gives a vision of how someday all who believe will call on Jesus and He will change their lives. Jesus is KEM's refuge, tower, and friend – his Savior, his power, his strength, the source of his joy, the love of his life and his provider – his hope when no one else is there.

Patti Labelle says because she accepted Jesus as her Savior, she does not have to fear. She knows she can still stand because of her relationship with Him. Ronald Isley told how he could not sing at one time, but because of Jesus' grace, he received another chance. If it had not been for Jesus, he would not be alive today. He encourages others to keep asking Jesus when they need a friend. When your brother or others are not there, Jesus will be.

This song is not only one of my favorite Christmas songs; it is also a praise and worship song for me. During some of my lowest times in my life, it ministered to me. It reminded me I can call on Jesus, the One who is my refuge, savior, protector, healer, the One who calms my spirit and who provides me grace and mercy.

Reflection: How can artists create meaningful lyrics that will help save souls and minister through powerful messages?

Prayer: Thank You, Lord, for the gift of hope. I pray we can continue to find solace and love in songs that have meaning and clarity about the Savior of the World! Amen.

Dr. Sheila R. Morris, Clarksville, TN
Retired Chicago Public Schools Principal

EIGHTH DAY OF CHRISTMAS

Embracing Darkness

One happy morning people will share ...

If I balanced just right on the counter, I could reach the light switch. Flipping the switch off and on, noticing how fast the light came and how long it took my eyes to adjust to the darkness was fun! I knew I wasn't supposed to play with it, but I was a curious child.

Darkness is surprising that way. Darkness is slow. Darkness takes adjustment. As a dark-skinned woman, I've learned to embrace my darkness in a culture that has not been hospitable to persons of dark hues.

Åke Lundqvist once wrote, "Darkness is not the absence of light. Light is diluted darkness. The speed of light is often talked about, in a kind of admiration. The speed of darkness is much slower. Darkness falls softly and quietly, as balm for the soul."

What can Advent reveal to us with its concentration of darkness? There is a sacred struggle in the darkness. We must wait for our eyes to adjust and see in the dark. During Advent, there is acute tension between the world as it is and the world as it could be. Artificial light distracts us from the growing darkness in the natural world. While the world says "go, buy, indulge," the Christmas story tells us to "wait, save, reflect." Maybe someday we will be comfortable in the darkness.

Reflection: As a child, were you afraid of the dark? How has your perception of darkness changed as you've grown?

Prayer: God, You sent Jesus to us to be light in the darkness, to show us a straight pathway to You. Thank You for the gift of light and life. Amen.

Rev. Virzola Law, Dallas, TX
Senior Minister, Northway Christian Church (Disciples of Christ),
Dallas, TX

NINTH DAY OF CHRISTMAS

Unexpected Gifts, Unexpected Blessings

... how silently the wondrous gift is given ...

In my loving family, two of my favorite people were my Aunt Quinnie and my Uncle Ed. Their wisdom and generosity made them a power couple to me. Every year at Christmas, they gave gifts to the family. During my senior year of high school, I made it clear that for Christmas I wanted a portable radio commonly referred to as a "boom box." I counted each day in anticipation of my marquee gift.

On Christmas day, Aunt Quinnie and Uncle Ed delivered their gifts. They handed me a wrapped box. Holding it in my hands, I paraded around, confident I was carrying my portable noisemaker. However, once I opened the box, I was shocked to discover no boom box inside. The power couple gave me an unexpected gift: a leather suitcase! While in that moment I did not appreciate the gift, my parents certainly did! Eventually, I found this suitcase to be a sturdy and reliable tool, one that I would use throughout my university and seminary days.

When I think about that suitcase and the life-enhancing investment Aunt Quinnie and Uncle Ed made in my future, I understand why my parents rejoiced when I received it. In Jesus, the Messiah gift-wrapped in cloths and placed in a manger, God made a life-enhancing investment in the future of humanity. Jesus would embody sturdy love and reliable hope as He presented good news to the poor, release to the captives, sight to the blind, and liberation of the oppressed. While it is not clear the shepherds understood the magnitude of God's great gift, the angel and the multitude of heavenly host got the message. They formed the world's first praise party, exclaiming, "Glory to God in the highest heaven, and on earth peace among those whom God favors!"

Reflection: How have unexpected gifts from God changed your life and given you joy?

Prayer: Wise and generous God, thank You for giving us good and perfect gifts, even ones we do not always understand or appreciate. Amen.

Rev. Dr. Jack Sullivan Jr.
Executive Director, Ohio Council of Churches

Finding Joy Even in Strange Predicaments and Places

... and wonders of His love ...

The arrival of the baby Jesus introduces a transformative joy amid strange predicaments and places. Like many commission stories in the Hebrew Bible, Jesus' arrival in swaddling clothes provides an opportunity to set things right. It brought God's redemptive plan to a Roman empire-informed world. The people in Jesus' day – and those who live with the complexities of our modern world – are introduced to the salvation and joy Christ offers. Where painful and disheartening realities become the norm, God through Christ transforms our human experience.

In Luke's gospel, Christ's arrival brings joy where political power was on display. The collection of taxes by Emperor Augustus was a sign of human authority. Jesus' birth in Bethlehem at the same time allowed God to challenge that authority. Jesus arrived during a strange predicament and context. While the owners of the fields and flocks lived comfortably in their homes, their slaves or hired help resided and worked outdoors. The angelic messenger's proclamation brought good news and joy to them. The transformative joy of Jesus includes lowly shepherds and rejects powers that exclude.

When we find ourselves struggling with challenges associated with the human condition, inequities, and overwhelming injustice in our world, remember the joy Christ brings. Maintaining peace and unity can become a daunting task. When war and violence seek to hijack our hope and rob us of our humanity, remember Christ's joy is all sufficient. Let this Advent season bring you the joy that transforms the strange predicaments and places you find yourself in.

Reflection: What strange realities are negatively impacting you, your family, and your community during this Advent season?

Prayer: Dear God, thank You for sending Jesus to offer joy to the world. Be a transformative presence in our midst. In Jesus' name, Amen.

Rev. Derrick L. Perkins Sr., St. Louis, MO
Senior Servant and Pastor, Centennial Christian Church
(Disciples of Christ), St. Louis, MO

ELEVENTH DAY OF CHRISTMAS

A Place Where Our Prayers Land

... the hopes and fears of all the years are met in thee tonight...

We all need a space, a person, or a community to experience liberating love – a place where our prayers land – a place vibrantly colored in affirmation and joy that is not fleeting, a place that offers shelter from our storms. We all need a Bethlehem signaling to our spirit and the world that we are seen by God and we matter. As it was in the time of Mary's unfathomable birth story, we have King Herod-type personalities determined to smother light that radiates truth and emboldens the afflicted. While at times it can seem discouraging that not enough has changed, wisdom cries out for us to see the hand of God working in the midst of brokenness. No matter the manner of force seeking to extinguish dreams of justice, peace, and love, Light will keep coming. It came to Bethlehem. It came for the ancestors. It is coming for us, and it will come for our children's children. The Light of Jesus will keep coming to the place of our prayers.

Written by Phillips Brooks and Lewis Redner around 1868, "O Little Town of Bethlehem" tells the story of a reckoning that approaches during the night. A vulnerable woman named Mary partners with darkness and light to give birth to change. Mary's baby was born in Bethlehem, a destination of human hope and holy dreams. The song helps us be less afraid of night because in "dark streets shineth the everlasting light." We can hear this song and be assured our prayers will land in a place where Love will show up and change everything.

Reflection: When did joy enter your life and afterwards you were never the same?

Prayer: Holy One, we remember with gratitude Your everlasting light and revolutionary love. Amen.

Rev. Monique Crain Spells, Brownsburg, IN
Vice President, Disciples Home Missions

TWELFTH DAY OF CHRISTMAS

Worshipping Beyond the Manger

Come and behold Him ...

All our carols and special Christmas music focus on the anticipated arrival of the promised Messiah. We share the stories in our Sunday School lessons, Christmas pageants, and programs. Every journey leads us to the manger, where all worship the baby as the incarnation of God's limitless love. The wise men from the East, seeking to connect their knowledge of the stars with the prophecies of Israel, were transformed by their encounter with the Holy Child, so much so they decided to go another way when they departed. They did not return to the way of the empire. Worship at the manger meant they could not return the same way or be the same people once they had encountered Jesus.

Christmas is certainly about the birth of the baby Jesus, but it is also about our hopes for how this baby, this Jesus, would change the world. All the Hebrew Bible prophecies about the Messiah speak about His ability to bring peace, love, justice, and transformation. When we worship at the manger, we are reminded our worshipful work in Jesus' Name must go beyond the manger. Jesus lived 33 years on earth, drawing to Himself the marginalized and forgotten. He taught, He healed, He made Himself available to those society shunned. He always pointed people to God, not to Himself. He did not come to establish a kingdom for His own benefit, but to teach us that the kindom of God is actually among us. How can we adore the baby and fail to love the people He came to save? Every act of justice, every act of liberation is an act of worship. Unless we are worshipping in this way beyond the manger, we are not truly disciples of Jesus. An invitation to worship is an invitation to discipleship. O, come let us adore him, Christ the Lord!

Reflection: How will you take your worship of the Lord beyond the manger?

Prayer: Lord Jesus, teach us to love as You loved, reaching out to all the people whom You love. Amen.

Rev. Teresa Hord Owens, Calumet City, IL
General Minister and President, Christian Church (Disciples of Christ)
in the United States and Canada
Minister Walter Owens Jr., Calumet City, IL
Minister of Music and Arts, Salem Baptist Church, Chicago, IL

A Promise of Hope and Peace

Someday at Christmas ... Hate will be gone and love will prevail ...

I have been accused of being an idealist – someone who clings to useless dreams that will never come true. I can't help it. Especially at Christmas, my heart expands to embrace all the love, hope, peace, and joy God has promised to send us through Jesus Christ. And just because I'm an idealist doesn't mean I'm not a realist as well. I know this world is not perfect. I know the sting of racism and the weariness of trying to prove my worth daily to doubters. I know people struggle with and sometimes succumb to their demons. I know there are wars going on and peace is only a faraway dream. But I can't help believing that someday – someday at Christmas – all the fighting will cease. All the hatred will be erased. All the tears will be wiped from our eyes and all the fears in our hearts will be swept away.

Throughout Advent, as we contemplate Jesus' birth and what it means, our hope, joy, peace, and love increase. On Christmas Day, we find contentment not in the gifts under our trees but in the knowledge that a Savior has been born to help us cope and overcome. Throughout Epiphany, the conviction grows stronger: God has made a promise of hope and peace to us, and God will keep that promise – just in time for you and me. Someday at Christmas, we will join together as brothers and sisters, singing the old song the angels sang for the shepherds: "Peace on earth, goodwill to all!" It's one prayer away.

Reflection: How do you cling to hope, peace, love, and joy in the midst of the sorrow and evil in the world?

Prayer: God, thank You for sending Jesus to us. He is our hope, our joy, and our peace now and forevermore. Amen.

Rev. Tanya J. Tyler, Alto, NM
Pastor, First Christian Church (Disciples of Christ), Ruidoso, NM